HAS THE EUROPEAN EXPERIMENT FAILED?

HAS THE EUROPEAN EXPERIMENT FAILED?

FERGUSON AND JOFFE VS.
MANDELSON AND COHN-BENDIT

THE MUNK DEBATE ON EUROPE

Edited by Rudyard Griffiths

ANANSI

This edition published in 2012 by
House of Anansi Press Inc.
110 Spadina Avenue, Suite 801
Toronto, ON, M5V 2K4
Tel. 416-363-4343
Fax 416-363-1017
www.houseofanansi.com

Distributed in Canada by
HarperCollins Canada Ltd.
1995 Markham Road
Scarborough, ON, M1B 5M8
Toll free tel. 1-800-387-0117

Distributed in the United States by
Publishers Group West
1700 Fourth Street
Berkeley, CA 94710
Toll free tel. 1-800-788-3123

The transcript of this debate seeks to be as close to a verbatim account of its proceedings as possible. Every reasonable effort has been made to verify the accuracy of the facts
and statistics presented in this debate.

House of Anansi Press is committed to protecting our natural environment.
As part of our efforts, the interior of this book is printed on paper that contains
100% post-consumer recycled fibres, is acid-free, and is processed chlorine-free.

16 15 14 13 12   1 2 3 4 5

Library and Archives Canada Cataloguing in Publication

Has the European experiment failed? : the Munk debate
on Europe / Daniel Cohn-Bendit . . . [et al.] ; edited by Rudyard
Griffiths.

(The Munk debates)
Issued also in electronic format.
ISBN 978-1-77089-228-6

1. European Union — History. I. Cohn-Bendit,
Daniel II. Griffiths, Rudyard III. Series: Munk debates

JN30.H373 2012   341.242'2   C2012-902575-5

Library of Congress Control Number: 2012937622

Cover design: Alysia Shewchuk
Text design and typesetting: Colleen Wormald
Transcription: Rondi Adamson

 Canada Council   Conseil des Arts
for the Arts   du Canada

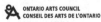 ONTARIO ARTS COUNCIL
CONSEIL DES ARTS DE L'ONTARIO

*We acknowledge for their financial support of our publishing program
the Canada Council for the Arts, the Ontario Arts Council, and the Government of Canada
through the Canada Book Fund.*

Printed and bound in Canada

 FSC
www.fsc.org
MIX
Paper from
responsible sources
FSC® C004071

 ANCIENT FOREST ™
FRIENDLY

CONTENTS

INTRODUCTION BY PETER MUNK

The crisis facing Europe is clear. For going on a generation, the majority of the national governments in the eurozone have spent more than they take in. The result is rapidly increasing debt and corresponding servicing costs as countries' deficits rise faster than their economies are expected to grow. This dangerous dynamic, and its pernicious social consequences, is nowhere more evident than in Greece, where the national public debt is fast approaching 200 percent of GDP. Taken as a whole, the eurozone currently has 1.1 trillion euros in debts due in 2012. And we must view these debts collectively, since the economic and political covenants of the European Union make it impossible for any individual country to restructure its debt unilaterally and still remain in the euro.

What lies at the core of the EU breakdown, and what we are witnessing, is the historic recalibration of the role of the modern state in real time. If the 2008 financial crisis showed us the failures inherent in the U.S. capital market model, the eurozone crisis is demonstrating the limits of the highly leveraged social welfare state. Through both crises, citizens of North America and Europe are struggling to reimagine what their governments can and should be. How much power should they have? How much money should they spend? And how should we draw the lines of accountability between citizens, the state, elected officials, and increasingly powerful transnational institutions? To top it off, this is all happening during a period of growing political uncertainty and unrest.

These issues formed the background for the ninth semi-annual Munk Debate, held at Roy Thomson Hall in Toronto, on Friday, May 25, 2012, before an audience of 2,700 and with over 3,000 people watching online. The resolution for the evening, "be it resolved the European experiment has failed," fostered our most spirited, and dare I say emotional, debate to date. Our debaters are each deeply invested in the still uncertain fate of the European project, which brought immediate consequence to the night's discussion.

Four exceptional debaters were assembled to tackle this critical issue. Arguing for the resolution were economic historian Niall Ferguson and German editor-publisher Josef Joffe. Arguing against the motion were EU parliamentarian Daniel Cohn-Bendit and former EU commissioner Lord Peter Mandelson.

Niall Ferguson is a celebrated Harvard professor of history, a *Daily Beast/Newsweek* columnist, and the author of numerous international bestselling books, including *The Ascent of Money: A Financial History of the World* and *Civilization: The West and the Rest*. For more than ten years, Ferguson argued, it has been the case that Europe has conducted an experiment in the impossible. A monetary union without labour market integration and without any fiscal federalism was bound to blow up. And the proof, said Ferguson, is in both the economic stagnation of the union and also in its geopolitical insignificance.

Debating with Niall Ferguson was Josef Joffe, the publisher of the prestigious German weekly *Die Zeit*. He is the author of numerous bestselling books on global politics, including *Überpower: The Imperial Temptation of America*. Europe has transcended a thousand years of war, Joffe argued, but twenty-seven nation-states will never grow into one. Europe is crumbling before our eyes, and its proudest achievement — the euro — is going to bury the union. In the end, Europe is broke, and Germany neither wants to, nor can afford to, pay for the rest. We must now hope, Joffe concluded, that the collapse of the economic union will not bring down European political ties.

Daniel Cohn-Bendit, who argued against the resolution, emerged on the European scene in the 1960s as a key leader of the student revolts in France. Half a century later, he remains fondly known as "Danny the Red," and serves as co-president of the Greens/European Free Alliance Group in the European Parliament. He also sits on the EU parliamentary committees for Economic and

Monetary Affairs and Constitutional Affairs. In the past, Cohn-Bendit has argued passionately that "we need a true democratic process for the renewal of Europe, in which the European Parliament plays a central role." The centrality of the democratic process must be seen in tandem with the EU's true political successes. Cohn-Bendit reminded us that this is a union born out of what was once the most murderous region in the world, and as a result, Europe is an objective that we must not disavow, despite the challenges of economic union.

Our final debater was Lord Peter Mandelson. Lord Mandelson has held numerous senior cabinet positions in the United Kingdom as a Labour MP under prime ministers Tony Blair and Gordon Brown. He was Great Britain's EU commissioner from 2004 to 2008, and is currently the chairman of Global Counsel, an international strategic advisory firm. Mandelson urged the audience to measure the European Union against a longer history and a bigger aim. While the euro is certainly in trouble, he argued, the eurozone is not the whole European project. The EU is based on a political idea that a group of once antagonistic countries can be more than the sum of its parts. It is this supranationalism that must remain the focus of our steady hand and be the topic of debate.

I was enthralled by the intellectual vigour and emotion of these four debaters. And because I grew up in Europe, this debate held particular significance for me.

As both Ferguson and Joffe argued persuasively, it may be simply too expensive to rescue the economies of

Greece, Spain, and possibly Italy, in addition to what has already been provided to Portugal and Ireland. In the end, it will come down to the German people, and the value they place on the economic union. Germany could possibly afford to bail out country after country, but it is questionable whether German savings can continue to fix the recurring problems of the European experiment. On the other hand, as Cohn-Bendit and Mandelson both argued, it may make more economic sense — despite the exorbitant costs — to save the union than reap the fallout of its collapse.

Perhaps the common currency was a mistake. And maybe the EU will be stronger if its member states revert to their national currencies. But either way, Europe is more than an economic union. It also unites the European peoples in a way they have never been united before. For a very long time, Europe was a place of tremendous violence — wars that my own family lived through. So, to me, the overriding importance of this project was that it eliminated local, regional, and international wars and conflicts that wiped out millions of families. We must never lose sight of the fact that it brought various peoples and cultures together into a political system capable of negotiating difference.

There are also lessons we can all learn from the problems facing Europe. At its core, we are seeing a challenge to the welfare state model. This is not just a conflict between countries, but a question of how countries are structured. The European crisis is the first manifestation of challenges facing the Western world as countries try to satisfy the ever-growing entitlement culture. It is a question of managing post-industrial economies, built on an industrial state model. And so the topic of this Munk Debate holds significance for those of us watching from afar. We are all observing with keen interest to see how — and if — the crisis will be resolved.

I would like to make one final comment about the debate itself. This Munk Debate was very emotional. Our debaters care passionately about the fate of the union, and about the prosperity and challenges that their countries face. For me, this is all the more reason to support spaces for the public exchange of conflicting ideas. I feel strongly that government policy needs to be bolstered by high-level public debate.

I think it is in all of our interests to elevate our awareness of, and engagement in, key issues that are currently at the forefront of global debate and discussion. In my mind, a hundred speeches will never match the power of one single debate amongst true thought leaders. In this kind of public forum, you are putting together people who have equal knowledge but vastly different policy views, which forces a defence of public policy too often missing from our civic discourse.

When we started holding these debates, our intention was a simple one: to highlight the finest thinkers debating the crucial issues facing our world. In that respect, we have again exceeded our expectations with this debate on the future of Europe. And for this I have to credit my Aurea Foundation Board and, more specifically, Rudyard

Griffiths and his team, who have done a wonderful job organizing and hosting these debates. I am proud of our Foundation's debate series, and, as ever, I am grateful to our debaters for an exceptional evening of discussion, excitement, emotion, and — yes — entertainment.

Has the European Experiment Failed?

Pro: Niall Ferguson and Josef Joffe
Con: Peter Mandelson and Daniel Cohn-Bendit

May 25, 2012
Toronto, Canada

THE MUNK DEBATE ON EUROPE

RUDYARD GRIFFITHS: Ladies and gentlemen, good evening. My name is Rudyard Griffiths. I'm the co-organizer of this debate series with my colleague, Patrick Luciani. It is my privilege to be your moderator once again.

I want to start by welcoming the worldwide audience who are watching tonight's debate live online, on web sites including Canada's leading news source, theglobeandmail.com. A warm hello also to the global TV and radio audience tuning into this debate: in Canada from the Business News Network (BNN), to CBC Radio's *Ideas*, or on CPAC (the Cable Public Affairs Channel), and on C-SPAN throughout the continental United States. And finally, hello to the 2,700 people who have once again filled Roy Thomson Hall to capacity for a Munk Debate.

We've had some stellar debates in this very hall. Who can forget that evening with Christopher Hitchens and

Tony Blair on religion's impact on the world? A year ago today Dr. Henry Kissinger, at eighty-two years of age, participated in his first public debate on this stage, eloquently arguing against China owning the twenty-first century. And just a matter of months ago, Nobel laureate Paul Krugman and former U.S. treasury secretary Larry Summers went head-to-head on the future of the North American economy.

As entertaining and engaging as those contests were, they did not have the urgency of tonight's debate. In the last month, the unthinkable has become the thinkable when it comes to the future of Europe. As early as mid-June 2012, Greece will form a new government that will have to decide in the coming months — by choice or out of necessity — if the country leaves the eurozone. Many observers have predicted that a Greek exit from the eurozone could cause a catastrophic spike in the borrowing costs of Spain and Italy — two of the world's largest debtor nations — and a bank run throughout the region. The result could be an implosion, both political and economic, of the European Union that would most likely plunge not only that continent, but North America and the world, back into recession.

But as dire as the scenarios presented in the media about Europe's future are right now, they need to be set against a record of real accomplishment and important history. The European Union, born out of the Second World War, now encompasses six decades of continuous history, some twenty-seven member states, twenty-three different languages, and an advanced economy that is responsible for a quarter of the world's economic output.

In the sweep of human history, Europe's institutions, its values, and its common goals are rightfully acknowledged as some of humankind's most important accomplishments. So I think we're all wondering tonight — we in this room and people around the world, especially people in Europe — whether the considerable strengths that Europe enjoys will allow it to survive its unprecedented crisis, and maybe even emerge from the other side stronger and more united; or, as two of our debaters will make the case this evening, is the eurozone crisis an expression of a series of deep and fatal flaws buried in the core of the euro itself that dooms it to failure?

Tonight, we are going to try and answer these important questions and tackle the big geopolitical question of our time. We will debate the motion: be it resolved, the European experiment has failed. Before introducing the all-star European cast of debaters that we've assembled, let me take a moment to recognize the organization that is solely responsible for staging these evenings. It's really thanks to its generosity and public-spiritedness that we have the opportunity, twice a year, to gather here in Toronto and listen to some of the world's brightest minds debate the big issues facing our country and the globe. Ladies and gentlemen, please join me in a round of applause for the co-founders of the Aurea Foundation, Peter and Melanie Munk.

Now, let's get our debate underway. Can I have a big round of applause for our two debaters arguing for tonight's motion, Niall Ferguson and Josef Joffe, and their formidable opponents, Daniel Cohn-Bendit and Lord Peter Mandelson.

Peter Munk joked with me earlier that we should rename these events the Ferguson Debates, since this is the third time Niall Ferguson has participated in a Munk Debate. But, brain cell for brain cell, he is one of the most formidable debaters of his generation. He's also a celebrated Harvard professor, a *Daily Beast/Newsweek* columnist, a documentary film impresario, and an internationally bestselling author.

Josef Joffe, also speaking in favour of tonight's motion, brings a vital perspective to this debate — the view of the German people on the fast-moving eurozone crisis. He is the publisher of the prestigious German weekly *Die Zeit*, Germany's equivalent of *Time* magazine or *Maclean's*. He is the author of numerous bestselling books on international affairs, including *Überpower: The Imperial Temptation of America*. His analysis of geopolitical events appears regularly in everywhere from the *New York Times* to *The New Republic* to the *London Times Literary Supplement*.

Let me introduce the debaters arguing against the motion. The life story of Daniel Cohn-Bendit is in many ways synonymous with the European experiment: born in France in 1945 to German-Jewish parents who had fled Nazi Germany, Mr. Cohn-Bendit burst upon the European scene in the 1960s as a key leader of the student revolts in France. Half a century later, he remains fondly known as "Danny the Red," and a highly influential voice in Europe, where he serves as co-president of the Greens/European Free Alliance Group in the European Parliament. He sits on the EU parliamentary committees on Economic and Monetary Affairs and Constitutional Affairs. He is also co-president of the respected Spinelli Group, a European parliamentary association dedicated to the federalist project in Europe.

Our final debater tonight, Lord Peter Mandelson, is one of Europe's most prominent and eloquent advocates for the cause of European federalism in the face of the current crisis. He has held numerous senior cabinet positions in the United Kingdom as a Labour MP under prime ministers Tony Blair and Gordon Brown. Most important to us tonight, he was Great Britain's EU commissioner from 2004 to 2008, a role that gave him an intimate understanding of the internal political and economic workings of Europe. Today he is the chairman of Global Counsel, an international strategic advisory firm. To top off his many talents, he is also a gifted writer. His autobiography, *The Third Man*, published in 2010, was a *Sunday Times* number-one bestseller for five consecutive weeks.

All 2,700 of you in attendance voted on the debate's resolution as you took your seats, which is a critical part of these events. We asked you to consider the motion: be it resolved the European experiment has failed. Your votes should give us a close idea of where public opinion is in this room right now. The numbers are interesting:

41 percent voted in favour of the motion, 37 percent were against it, and 22 percent were undecided. So public opinion is split.

On the second question on your ballot, we asked you whether or not you are open to changing your vote, depending on what you hear at this debate. Wow — this is an undecided audience! Ninety percent of you would change your minds in the next hour and forty-five minutes. Only 10 percent of you have your minds completely made up. Ladies and gentlemen, this debate is very much in play.

One last housekeeping point that we stick to at every debate: our debaters will have six minutes for their opening remarks and three minutes for their closing remarks. I now call on Niall Ferguson for the first opening statement. Sir, you have six minutes.

NIALL FERGUSON: Thank you. *Merci. Mersi. Grazie. Gracias. Grazzi. Go raibh maith agat. Dziekuje. Danke. Aitäh. Köszönöm. Multumesc. Dêkuji. Paldies. Ačiū. Dakujem. Obrigado. Hvala. Dank u. Kiitti. Blagodaria. Merci villmahl. Efharisto.* And my personal favourite, *tak.*

There are twenty-three ways of saying thank you in the European Union, and I think that in itself illustrates why the European experiment has ended in failure. Do you remember those experiments that you used to do as a kid with a chemistry set? You would keep adding chemicals, one after the other, to see what would finally produce an explosion. That's what they did in Europe. It started with six; that wasn't enough. It went to nine . . . nothing.

Ten . . . a little bit of smoke, nothing more. Twelve . . . nothing. Fifteen . . . still nothing. Twenty-five . . . beginning to bubble. Twenty-seven . . . explosion!

I'm absolutely certain that Lord Mandelson and Daniel Cohn-Bendit will tell you that the European experiment has succeeded because there has been peace in Europe since it began in the 1950s. Can we just knock that on the head? European integration has had absolutely nothing to do with peace in Europe since World War II; that has been the achievement of NATO [the North Atlantic Treaty Organization]. The creation of the European Union was not about war and peace, otherwise there would have been a European Defence Community, and that was vetoed by the French National Assembly in 1954.

Europe has to be judged in economic terms, since its own terms have always been economic. And how did it do? In the 1950s the economy of integrated Europe grew at 4 percent. In the 1960s, it was about the same. In the 1970s, growth was 2.8 percent; in the 1980s, it slid to 2.1 percent; in the 1990s, it was only 1.7 percent: and so on, down to zero.

As European integration has proceeded, its growth has declined. The share of Europe in global GDP has fallen since 1980 from 31 percent to just 19 percent. Since 1980 the EU has grown faster than the United States in only nine out of thirty-two years. Never has its unemployment rate been lower than the U.S. unemployment rate.

Are any of you investors? What were the worst

equity markets of the last ten years? They were Greece, Ireland, Italy, Finland, Portugal, the Netherlands, and Belgium — the worst in the world. And on top of all of this, we have monetary union — the ultimate experiment gone wrong.

We warned them, ladies and gentlemen. We said, if you have a monetary union without labour market integration and without any fiscal federalism, it will blow up. I predicted that in 2000. It is happening in real time, in a chemistry lab, on the other side of the Atlantic.

But this was also a political experiment gone wrong. Do you know what that experiment was? The experiment was to see if Europeans could be forced into an even closer union — despite their wishes — by economic means because the political means failed.

And when the European peoples voted against further integration, their respective governments were told to try again. It happened to the Danes in 1992, and to the Irish twice: in 2001 and again in 2008. Their citizens gave the wrong answer in the referendum, so the governments just held another one. This tells you something about why this experiment has failed — it has failed because it has lost political legitimacy. And we see this not only in Greece but in government after government across Europe. Thirteen have fallen since this crisis began two years ago, and more will follow in the months to come.

Finally, the European experiment has been a geopolitical failure. The European Union was supposed to act as counterweight to the United States. Do you remember Jacques Poos's 1991 "hour of Europe" speech announcing that Europe was going to solve the war in Bosnia?[1] Yes, that was supposed to be in 1991. But one hundred thousand people died in that war and 2.2 million were displaced, and the conflict didn't end until the United States finally stepped in and sorted out the mess.

Henry Kissinger famously asked, "Who do I call when I want to call Europe?" The answer came several years later: you call Baroness Ashton of Upholland.[2] Nobody had ever heard of her, nor had they ever heard *from* her. Ladies and gentlemen, you're Canadians. You know how hard it is to run a federal system with just ten provinces and only two languages; that's why you will understand more readily than most people why the European experiment, with twenty-seven countries and a staggering twenty-three languages, has ended in ignominious failure. Thankfully, here in Canada I only have to use two or maybe three words now. Thank you and *merci*.

---

[1] Economist Jacques Poos held a number of senior cabinet posts in Luxembourg from 1976 to 1999. As foreign minister, he was president of the Council of the European Union on three separate occasions (in 1985, 1991, and 1997). In 1991, while on his way to negotiations aimed at resolving the growing crisis in the former Yugoslavia, Poos declared: "This is the hour of Europe. It is not the hour of the Americans . . . If one problem can be solved by the Europeans, it is the Yugoslav problem."

[2] Catherine Ashton, Baroness Ashton of Upholland, the European Union's High Representative of the Union for Foreign Affairs and Security Policy. She is also vice-president of the European Commission.

RUDYARD GRIFFITHS: Daniel Cohn-Bendit, you're up next.

DANIEL COHN-BENDIT: Good evening. I can say it only in English. You know, I have to calm myself. I've never heard such stupid things! And I will tell you why. My parents fled from Germany in 1933. My father was a lawyer, and he would have been arrested after the burning of the Reichstag. Then they had to flee to the south of France because my mother and father were Jews. I was conceived after the landing of the troops in Normandy. Nine months later, in April 1945, I was born.

Imagine if I had said to my parents that in fifty years there would be no military forces between France and Germany, except those that are part of NATO; that there would be no troops, no soldiers in all of Europe; and imagine that I said you could travel anywhere on the continent. My parents would have said, "We have a problem. We have a kid who's speaking too early, and he's speaking nonsense."

European integration was a big civilizational step. Many of the world's most destructive political experiments originated in Europe: we created colonialism; we created fascism; and we created communism. The continent was the most murderous region in the world. We started two world wars, and the fighting had to end. We could not continue on this path, and we decided that the best idea was to form a union that allowed the European peoples to do business together and exchange goods. They took the big step when they created the European Union.

Then communism fell. And then there was the generation of François Mitterrand and Helmut Kohl. Mitterrand said — and Margaret Thatcher agreed — that you have to deepen European integration; you have to deepen it so that there would no longer be a hegemonic state in Europe; so that there would be no more fighting, and so that countries would have to work together — they could fight in a parliament, but no longer on the battlefield.

Then they created the euro. And, yes, the euro is in trouble. But having a union is difficult. A common state like Europe has never been created without war. And, Niall, you are right about Bosnia; I personally supported the idea of a European intervention. But we have to take responsibility for the continent. Look at the situation in Europe today; the nation-states can't take on the problems of the crisis — the economic fiscal crisis and climate change — alone. At this rate no European state will be in the G8 in thirty years. Only Europe can defend the European Union.

Yes, the process is challenging. But I prefer Europeans having difficulties speaking to one another than being at war together. The language of war is universal, so this argument about all the language barriers is crazy. We have translators. We can make it work. Come to the European Parliament and you can see for yourself.

Joining the European Union is the dream of many countries. If it is as bad as you suggest, then why have countries voted to get in? Why, after the fall of the Wall, did the Polish want to join? What about the Hungarians?

They wanted to be part of the EU because it's the future. Saying it's the future doesn't mean it's not difficult; it doesn't mean that we can't have backlash. But I strongly believe that if we don't continue European integration, the European nation-states will be in trouble because of their ageing societies.

We need to stay together to defend ourselves. The European Union is an umbrella that allows us to defend our vision of how to live together, and we were able to achieve this without war. As you know, the United States of America came together after a civil war. Our civil wars were two world wars, and then we Europeans learned to work together. I know discussion can be more complicated, but I will tell you an old Jewish joke: if you have two solutions, always choose the third. And this is Europe.

RUDYARD GRIFFITHS: Up next, speaking for the resolution, Josef Joffe.

JOSEF JOFFE: I have to start by correcting my friend Niall. He's wrong about the phone number. There *is* a phone number. The phone number is Catherine Ashton's. You call the phone number and then you get a computer voice: for Germany, press 1; for France, press 2 — that tells you where Europe is at.

Let me say something else. I think Europe was a wonderful idea. After all, Zeus, the god of gods, risked his marriage by running off with Europa — a woman he was smitten with. And Ovid, the Roman poet, sings,

"Till in the open sea he bore his prize . . . her right hand grasped a horn, the other leant upon his back."

Europe was also a wonderful idea several eons later when it decided to unify after the two most murderous wars in history. What a magnificent story. First, six nations got together by integrating coal and steel. Next, they slowly created a common market for goods, capital services, and people; democracy followed à la Cohn-Bendit with a European Parliament, and finally they introduced the euro, which meant no more francs, pesetas, and drachmas. Now there are twenty-seven member states. The euro reigns from Portugal to the borders of Poland. Now what would come next? Of course, the United States of Europe.

DANIEL COHN-BENDIT: Yes!

JOSEF JOFFE: Wrong! Europe is crumbling before our eyes. The grandest experiment since the thirteen American colonies became *E Pluribus Unum* now faces its most deadly crisis. Why has this seemingly inexorable march of progress ground to a halt?

Think about integration as a mountain climb in the Rockies or on the Alps. In the beginning or in the foothills it is nice and easy. As we rise, the ascent gets tougher and the air gets thinner. Finally we reach the sheer cliff, the north face of the Eiger, in Switzerland, for example — a cliff that forms the core of national sovereignty.

This is where we are today, with the euro, our proudest achievement, about to bury us. We have gone too far, so what do you do next? There are only three ways: you retreat, stop, or attack. Do you attack the summit and climb to the United States of Europe? "Just look at your party of seventeen," this mountain growls, "all stragglers, miscreants, cripples, free-riders." And because this is a very educated mountain, he would add that there is no true unification without war, where the strongest element forces the rest into a single state.

That is what happened in Italy and Germany, and of course, as Danny already said, in the United States, where the civil war was actually a war of national unification. There will be no such war in Europe, and thank God for that. There is no Bismarck or Lincoln in Europe's future. And Frau [Angela] Merkel is no Bismarck, of course.

But what does this deadly crisis tell us? It says that you can't go to the summit unless you are both willing and able. Except you are neither of those things and nor will you ever be because: (a) you can't and will not give up the biggest chunk of democratic sovereignty, which is the power to tax and spend; and (b) you don't belong in the same climbing party to begin with. Just two or three or four of you have the discipline and the stamina to keep going. The rest are overweight, lame, or out of breath.

So let's bring it down from the mountain metaphor. The political point is that Europe is broke, and Germany neither wants nor is able to pay for the rest. Even France is broke. Furthermore, the stragglers don't want to go back to camp, to get into shape through a very painful domestic regimen that has already killed so many of their governments.

The deepest problem is the stubborn tenacity of the nation-state, which will not submit when the core of its sovereignty is at stake. Money, as the Germans say, is where a friendship stops, and so does integration. The EU is not cavorting in the foothills anymore. It's facing the north face of the Eiger.

So is Europe history now? We don't know yet. But we do know one thing: that the experiment has failed in one sense because that wonderful dream from the 1950s — of up, up, and away — has collided with the nasty reality of the nation-state that will not fade away. And if truth be told, how many Frenchmen, Italians, Germans, Poles, and so on, will want to part with two thousand years of history? Who wants to be ruled from Brussels rather than from his or her own capital?

Let me conclude with a prayer. Let's pray that the inevitable crash of the euro, the most ambitious part of the experiment, will not bury the rest of the union. And let's plead with Zeus to save Europa from the angry seas and set her down at a cozy little harbour because Europe cannot conquer the sea that is the nation-state. But if she drowns, Canada and the United States will not flourish. Amen. Thank you.

RUDYARD GRIFFITHS: Our final debater, speaking against the motion, is Lord Peter Mandelson. Sir, you have six minutes.

PETER MANDELSON: Thank you very much. First of all, I must take Niall and Josef up on their sneering remarks about Catherine Ashton. Two days ago the five permanent members of the United Nations Security Council, along with Germany — the great powers — went into very serious negotiations with Iran about the development of their nuclear capability. Who was leading the great powers? Who was leading the Security Council permanent members? No, Niall. No, Josef. It was not Hillary Clinton, it was Catherine Ashton. So let's have a little less sneering, please, and a little more seriousness.

Tonight is an opportunity to see an Englishman, a Scotsman, a German, and a sort of Frenchman knock each other around on stage. It sounds like the beginning of a bad joke, really, which is what I understand many of you think Europe and its currency are at the moment. But Danny and I are going to ask you to step back and look at a more serious and bigger picture. We are going to ask you to measure the European Union against a longer history and a bigger aim. Before we can define failure in this motion we have to know what we are talking about.

The EU's currency zone is certainly in trouble, and it's sending out distress signals. I don't deny that. But the eurozone is not the whole European project. That project started over six decades ago when people realized that the whole in Europe could, should, and would be bigger than the sum of its parts; that by pooling elements of our sovereignty and decision-making we can achieve things that would not be possible if we remained a collection of relatively small and rather combative nation-states. In doing that, we have put centuries of conflict in Europe behind us, which is not a small accomplishment.

We have also ended the division of Europe, east and west, and successfully anchored all of the post-Soviet states and the post-dictatorship states of Spain, Greece, and Portugal in a system of values of irreversible democratic and human rights — no small achievement. And we have created the world's largest economic space of its kind.

In creating this unique model of supranationalism, we've succeeded in doing what has never been attempted or done before in any other part of the world. This union has become absolutely central to European life — our commerce, our diplomacy, our security, and our policy coordination in so many different areas. I don't think either Niall or Josef could argue with this achievement if they were actually being serious. So presumably they agree that if the EU did not exist, European states would actually want to invent something today very much like it.

I don't think we can even write off the euro as a failure yet, although the currency union is certainly flawed. It's now clear that two decades ago Europe started to run economically before it could walk politically. This is not, in my view, because we were over-ambitious; rather, it was because we were actually not ambitious *enough*. We weren't ambitious enough to create the political institutions and machinery needed to make economic and monetary union work.

Now we debate the question: is this failure of the eurozone permanent? In my view the failure is one of design and execution, not concept and principle. The other side will tell you that the whole thing is going to hell in a handcart. But there is a workable version of a single currency; the question is whether Europe has the political will to implement it.

So, yes, a serious stumble and, yes, a serious flaw in design. But failure for the whole European project? I would argue not. It's very easy to be a historian, like Niall, talking about the past, looking through your rear-view mirror the entire time. But for a politician and a minister, I'm afraid, you have to be a little bit more practical and a little bit more serious.

So has Europe failed? I would say it is just too soon to know. Could Europe fail? Of course it could. But *must* Europe fail? Absolutely not. Thank you very much.

RUDYARD GRIFFITHS: Well done, gentlemen, a very strong opening to the debate. And I think you've flushed out something important, which is how this audience chooses to define the European experiment. Is it the euro? Is it a larger civilizational experiment? That's going to be up to you to decide when you pick up your second ballot after the debate, and for those of you voting online right now.

The next phase of this debate is to have these speakers engage each other directly. Niall, as the first to speak, I'm going to come to you. What have you heard from the opposing side that you fundamentally disagree with and that you think they've got wrong from A to Z? I'm then going to ask them to rebut your point.

NIALL FERGUSON: Exactly as I predicted, Danny Cohn-Bendit fell into the trap of attributing Europe's peace to the European Union, to the process of European integration. Europe's peace, since the 1940s, has had almost nothing to do with the process of European integration, which has been primarily economic. It is not the institutions of the EU that made peace. NATO and the division of Europe during the Cold War did that. The only attempt to make European institutions concerned with military affairs failed in 1954 because France voted it down in the National Assembly.

Europe's issues are economic. And I noted that neither Danny nor Peter addressed my point that, in economic terms, Europe has failed to deliver. I've just come back from Europe. Maybe you live there and so don't notice, but there is a massive economic crisis unfolding on the continent because of the failed project of monetary union. What are you going to say about that?

DANIEL COHN-BENDIT: I will tell you two things. First, one of Europe's biggest achievements is that the European peoples came together — NATO isn't the only reason there is peace on the continent. Because if the people of Europe hadn't united and become essentially borderless then there wouldn't be peace. This is one achievement and you can't deny it.

I want to continue on economic failure. When German reunification took place, Jacques Delors [former president of the European Commission] put together a plan to have Germany integrate via fluid cash exchange. It was the European states united that helped the Germans with reunification.

Why else would all the eastern European countries want to join the EU? When Poland entered the union, it was European financing that helped the country emerge from communism, and today the Polish majority agree on this point. Such was the case in many countries; Europe has been instrumental in their success.

On the economy, Josef and Niall were right on one point: we must have both a political and fiscal approach. If not, we will be in trouble. It is time to be ambitious, and we have to come together.

RUDYARD GRIFFITHS: Let me come back to Josef and ask him to follow up on what Danny's saying. Why is a United States of Europe not a conceivable outcome of this crisis, considering the cost of collapse and what would ensue?

JOSEF JOFFE: The problem with Danny and Peter's opinion is that they assume the desire is there; that if we had political will, if we had political union, then we would overcome all the problems. But that is putting the cart before the horse. The problem is that isn't the reality, and we have to figure out why we don't have these two things. None of us — the Brits, least of all, by the way — wants to give up national sovereignty.

We don't want to be ruled by Brussels. Neither do *you* want to be ruled by Brussels, nor you. Certainly none of us wants that. And that's why, when we get to the north face of the Eiger, we can't keep going.

RUDYARD GRIFFITHS: Lord Mandelson, you come in on this point. Why would countries set aside some of these final key pieces of their sovereignty in return for a larger Europe that would come out of this crisis, in your view, stronger and more united?

PETER MANDELSON: I don't think they do have to set aside their sovereignty, as you put it; I don't think they need to cease being nation-states. They don't have to cease to be Britain, or France, or Germany. The Spanish don't have to stop being Spanish. And the Belgians will continue to muddle through as they do. We're not asking people to give up their nation-states. What we are observing is that Europeans have chosen to see their states and their governments pool their sovereignty and their decision-making abilities in respect to certain key areas of their lives. And the most important part of their lives is their economic life — how businesses are created, how jobs are generated, how wealth is created in Europe.

Europe is far from being broke. We still represent 25 percent of global GDP and we don't have anything like the debt mountain of the United States. Are you suggesting that because the United States has debt, they are broke? Of course, they're not broke. The argument for a single market, which is the biggest single economic space or block of its kind, is twofold.

The first point is that by enabling businesses to trade across a single market of 500 million people, you allow businesses to grow in ways that would otherwise not be possible if they were limited to their own countries and if they faced a range of twenty-seven different sets of regulatory laws and policies preventing them from trading freely across that single market.

Second, why was I admitted in Washington, or Beijing, or Moscow, or Delhi, or Brasilia, when I was the European trade commissioner? It's not because I am British, it's not because I am Peter — charming, articulate, lucid; it's because I represented Europe, a market of 500 million people. And those countries, with their businesses, job creation, and their imports and exports want to get access to our 500-million-strong market.

If I was simply knocking on the door because I was Luxembourgian; if I was simply knocking on the door because I was Belgian; even if I was knocking on the door because I was German — representing a relatively small market and a small population — I would not get a hearing. I would not have the clout. I would not be able to negotiate with the force with which I was able to negotiate as the European trade commissioner representing the entirety of the EU — that's reality.

RUDYARD GRIFFITHS: Let's hear the other side. Niall, you're up.

NIALL FERGUSON: Number one, it's all very well for you to sing the praises of the European Union as an economic area, but it is actually 19 percent of global GDP, and shrinking fast. Why is it shrinking? It is shrinking because Europe is inflicting a completely man-made, avoidable recession on itself. Why is it doing that? It is happening because of the faulty design of the European monetary union. Who designed it? People like Peter, who designed it in the 1980s.

PETER MANDELSON: Lovely! I'd love to take responsibility.

NIALL FERGUSON: The design flaw existed from the outset. The Delors Report from 1989 claimed that for all of this to work, for the monetary union to work, there would have to be central control over national budgets, which never happened. Remember the Stability and Growth Pact?[3] Every single member of the eurozone violated it. The Greeks cooked the books, but they weren't the only ones. Even the Germans violated their own rules, and the net result has been an economic disaster. Do you know what the youth unemployment rate is in Spain today? Fifty percent. You need to put a face on it, Peter, because it is not your problem. But I can tell you that young Spaniards are in trouble and they are fleeing Europe.

---

[3]   The agreement of the EU member states to maintain the economic and monetary union; it was proposed by German finance minister Theo Waigel in 1995, and established in 1997.

PETER MANDELSON: Do you think that the banking crisis might have had something to do with the fact that there is 25 percent unemployment in Spain? Where have you been?

NIALL FERGUSON: I'll tell you where I've been. In February of 2009 I was in this city [Toronto], and I said the European banking crisis was going to be as bad as the American banking crisis because the leverage issue was just as serious and the whole of the balance sheets was bigger. I've said that repeatedly since early 2009, and what has been done in Europe? Nothing. Do you know what your policy was — you and your fellow eurocrats? You just kicked the can down the road for month after month after month.

RUDYARD GRIFFITHS: I want to get everybody's voice in here, so I'm going to give Josef two minutes and then I'm going to give Danny two minutes, because we're going to move onto questions next.

JOSEF JOFFE: You have accused us of having no arguments. Let me turn this around and point out that you said something that is typical of all failed experiments, from socialism to the EU. The theory is okay; the concept is okay; the problem is just in the design or execution. You remind me of the French NATO officer who comes to NATO for the first time and says, "This works very nicely in practice, but will it also work in theory?" The theory of European integration is wrong.

And I can tell that it is wrong by the way you argue. You spend so much time arguing for this wonderful economic space, but nobody challenges this wonderful economic space.

We are talking about whether Europe can acquire the will and the wherewithal to go to the next step. And if you want an economic model, look at NAFTA [North American Free Trade Agreement] between Canada, Mexico, and the United States: it's almost as big as Europe. They have free trade, but who wants to get together politically? Do Canadians want to form a political union with the United States or with Mexico? You've now made a case for an economic free trade zone, but that's not what we are debating in this room.

NIALL FERGUSON: Hear, hear.

RUDYARD GRIFFITHS: Danny, come in on this, because you're sitting in the European Parliament every day; you're at the proverbial mountain face there. Why do you think we can have a greater level of integration when we are seeing a lot of political disunity in Europe right now?

DANIEL COHN-BENDIT: We have European laws for the governance of the European economy and the banking system, and for how economic stability should be realized by all the member countries. Before the Stability and Growth Pact, these were decided by the European Parliament, but since the first of January 2012, they are decided by law. And you are right — when the Germans and the French break the Pact, it is ineffective.

RUDYARD GRIFFITHS: I'll turn to your opponents. Is there anything final that you would like to say before we go to questions?

NIALL FERGUSON: Yes. This is very simple. What you've heard is that Europe has to go to the next step in order to sort out the crisis. There has to be some central control of fiscal decisions at the national level. That is federalism, as you know from your own Canadian experience. The trouble is that's not what Europeans want. Indeed, when a treaty for European federalism was put to referendums in 2005, it was rejected by the French and the Dutch, and then abandoned.

So what you are calling for — a transition to the United States of Europe or a Federal Republic of Europe — doesn't have political legitimacy, which is why it hasn't happened. So your solution is a non-solution; it isn't going to work. The Germans are not going to vote to make those financial transfers to the other countries.

PETER MANDELSON: I'm confused about something, Niall. I've been listening to what you've been saying this evening. But I also read an article that you wrote in the *Financial Times* earlier this month. You were talking about the repairs that are needed to the eurozone, but nowhere did you write that they were impossible to implement. You talked about the need for a new fiscal compact; you argued that the ECB [European Central Bank] needs to help national banks directly; you mentioned the creation of eurobonds; you discussed joint and several liability for eurozone sovereign debt. Your only complaint was that it was taking Europe longer to create a fiscal federalism than it had taken the United States.

NIALL FERGUSON: Exactly.

PETER MANDELSON: You finished your article with a great flourish, quoting the Spanish philosopher José Ortega y Gasset. You said, "Europe is the solution," not the problem.* Now who is the true Niall Ferguson, may I ask?

NIALL FERGUSON: Since that article was published —

PETER MANDELSON: May 2, 2012 — just three weeks ago!

NIALL FERGUSON: Since that article was published, have you heard anything from the German government to suggest that any of those things are going to happen?

PETER MANDELSON: You've said the opposite of what you were arguing three weeks ago!

RUDYARD GRIFFITHS: This has certainly been a lively debate. Do we all agree that we want to hear questions

* In his 1910 essay "La pedagogía social como programa político" [Social pedagogy as a political program], Ortega (1883–1955) made his famous statement that "Spain is the problem, Europe is the solution."

from the audience? The first question is going to come from a good friend: CBC's senior business correspondent, reporter, and on-air personality Amanda Lang.

AMANDA LANG: My question is for Niall. I'm going to build on Josef's analogy of the mountain climb. I think mountain climbers would tell you that as many people die on the way down as on the way up. So the question is a very practical one: is it not better, more sensible, in this time of crisis, to press on to closer monetary and political union, rather than retreat, with all the losses that might entail?

NIALL FERGUSON: One point on that, Amanda. I've been arguing for some time now that these steps need to be taken to avoid a major banking crisis comparable in its magnitude to the crisis of 1931.

PETER MANDELSON: Well done, I agree!

DANIEL COHN-BENDIT: We agree!

NIALL FERGUSON: But the problem is that since I wrote that article, nothing has come from Berlin but a single word: *nein*. She [Angela Merkel] says, no. And here is the problem. You can say thank you in twenty-three different languages, but when it comes to saying no, there is only one language that really matters, and that is German.

The single biggest problem is that the proposition before the German government and people is: do you want to take the next step to a federal Europe? And when the Germans look at how much that is going to cost them, they say no. Although I would very much like to avoid the breakup right now, I've seen no sign that the German government, from a domestic point of view, is willing to take the massive political risk that would be involved in eurobonds. This is not going to happen. That is the significance of the piece you quoted from, Peter, and you know it.

RUDYARD GRIFFITHS: Peter, you spoke last, so Danny, go ahead.

DANIEL COHN-BENDIT: I just wanted to tell Niall that they have taken a poll in Germany on the question: "Do you want Germany to take on more debt to invest in Europe?" And a big majority said yes.

JOSEF JOFFE: No. Danny's Green and Red friends said they wanted to take on more debt, but not the nation as a whole.

Can I also answer the initial question? First of all, I want to say something about Ortega y Gasset. You don't understand, Peter, how much you played into Niall's hands with that quote, because Ortega said that "Europe is the solution" about 150 years ago. It makes the point that this wonderful desire the two of you share in your dream-like approach to politics does not work. Otherwise something would have happened in these 150 years.

DANIEL COHN-BENDIT: Excuse me, but maybe sometimes *you* should dream.

RUDYARD GRIFFITHS: We're going to go to the next question right now. We have Thrasy Petropoulos, live on Skype from Athens, Greece — the frontline of the eurozone crisis. He is the managing editor of the leading English-language daily in Greece, the *Athens News*. Thrasy has been watching the global web stream live. What have you heard tonight that you fundamentally disagree with in terms of what these two teams have presented?

THRASY PETROPOULOS: Well, it's interesting. I'm living in a country that might soon find itself outside of the eurozone. So I suppose I have more of a comment than a question. I'd like to know, given that there are ten members of the EU that are not in the eurozone, what life do you think there would be for the European Union without the euro? Given that the union is built on freedom of movement and trade, and that there are so many issues like immigration and the environment that are going to affect all of us, how will the EU work if more countries abandon the euro?

NIALL FERGUSON: So, can Greece leave the euro and remain in the European Union as, for example, the United Kingdom does?

RUDYARD GRIFFITHS: Let's deal with the first part of this question. Can Greece exit the eurozone? Can you have a "Grexit" and still have those other countries hold together in a single unit? Can it survive?

PETER MANDELSON: On the basis of opinion polls, 70 to 80 percent of the Greek people say they want to remain in the euro. I think they know full well that if they were to come out of the eurozone now and revert to their own national currency it would, in all probability, sink like a stone. Inflation would soar. The sovereign default, as well as the default on euro-denominated contracts — both within the country and externally — would create a lawyers' paradise; it would create extraordinary economic and social chaos in Greece. That is why, for Greece's sake, we have to move heaven and earth to keep it in the euro.

DANIEL COHN-BENDIT: Look, I am critical of the Greek government because I think the austerity measures are too strong and the population can't stand them; but if Greece leaves the eurozone, the new government will have no money to pay back their debts and there will be an uprising. And what happens with population uprisings, as we know from history, is that the military will take over. There are big risks involved, and I think we really should do more to keep Greece in the euro.

We have to try and help ease these difficulties because it could be very dangerous otherwise. The EU countries with their own currencies outside the euro, like Denmark, have national currencies that move in sync with the euro. So there are a lot of countries that are not in the

European monetary union, but are completely linked to the euro because they are economically linked to Europe. The euro can create stability even in difficult times. Look at the United States: the dollar stabilized California and New York, for example, when they had no money.

JOSEF JOFFE: How can you say that, given how the euro is tumbling? It is the strongest force for instability in our lives. I don't want any Brit to tell me about what the euro is and what it should do, because it isn't their issue. Otherwise, Britain would have been in the eurozone instead of gloating, "Thank God we never got into it!"

RUDYARD GRIFFITHS: What Danny and Peter are saying is important: that Europe will do whatever it takes to keep Greece in Europe regardless of whether or not there is a new government that will reject the austerity measures. Will Germany sign on to that?

JOSEF JOFFE: I will gladly do it if you tell me where the money will come from. Will we get it from the Brits, who are broke? Will we get it from the French, who are broke, whose national debt has escalated from 35 percent of GDP to 90 percent in twenty years? Will we get it from the great state of Luxembourg? Or maybe from Spain, which is also broke? Where will we get the money? If you tell me where the money is, we can talk business.

NIALL FERGUSON: That's a really good question. Where will the money come from, Danny? Where will the money come from to keep Greece in?

DANIEL COHN-BENDIT: The money will come from eurobonds.

NIALL FERGUSON: But the Germans are saying no.

DANIEL COHN-BENDIT: The Germans will not say no.

PETER MANDELSON: Two weeks ago, I was in the German Chancellery, meeting with the person responsible for Europe. The other month I visited with the president of the Deutsche Bundesbank in Frankfurt. Prior to that, I had been to the Ministry of Finance in Berlin. On not one occasion did any official — president, councillor, or whomever he was — ever say to me that Germany did not want to become part of the solution of the eurozone crisis. And secondly —

NIALL FERGUSON: So what did they tell you? Did they tell you what they were going to do? Because I read the *Financial Times* too, and every statement that has come out of Berlin since I wrote that article has been negative about eurobonds and negative about using funds to bail out —

PETER MANDELSON: You're wrong, actually. Do you want the answer? Why do you think it is, Niall, that they keep claiming that they're not prepared to do anything, and yet an extra 500 billion euro exposure has come onto the balance sheet of the Bundesbank?

NIALL FERGUSON: Because they can't stop that; because they can't prevent it.

PETER MANDELSON: No, because they've agreed to it, Niall. They want to be part of the solution.

NIALL FERGUSON: No, that is not how it works and you know it. Their Target2 liabilities, which are now hundreds of millions of euros, were automatically run up under the terms of the monetary union. The Germans didn't have a say. It happened automatically. And they're extremely worried about it —

PETER MANDELSON: I thought you said the Germans could always say no. But the point is they haven't said *nein*, they've said *ja*.

NIALL FERGUSON: No, Peter, that is not correct.

RUDYARD GRIFFITHS: We're going to go to another question. This one is important because, as Niall mentioned, this crisis affects a lot of young Europeans. There is 50 percent unemployment amongst eighteen- to twenty-five-year-olds in both Greece and Spain. So I'm going to go to Melanie Greene, a master's student in International Affairs at the Munk School.

MELANIE GREENE: Thank you. I'd like to ask the debaters tonight what hope, if any, do young people in Europe have for the future, given the extremely high youth unemployment across the continent?

RUDYARD GRIFFITHS: Danny, why don't you weigh in on that? Your political career began as a young man on the streets of Paris. Was unemployment at 50 percent back then?

DANIEL COHN-BENDIT: I have two things I want to mention. First, in the last European Council meeting, they approved measures to take 25 billion euros from the European budget to start new youth programs in Spain, Italy, and Greece. Second, the German Chancellor and François Hollande — the newly elected French president — agreed to put together a proposal for a special program to combat youth unemployment across Europe that would be discussed at the end-of-June summit. And Ms. Merkel said that Germany will participate as much as they possibly can on this issue. The European Parliament is on the right track by putting this proposition forward, since youth unemployment is a real concern.

RUDYARD GRIFFITHS: Niall, you're a historian; you've looked at revolutions throughout history. Is there a tipping point? Does 50 percent unemployment in that demographic suggest that social instability is now just seething beneath the surface?

NIALL FERGUSON: When I arrived in Barcelona just a few days ago, it took me over an hour to get to the hotel because of the student demonstrations; this isn't only happening in Montreal. The mood is very bleak. And it is very bleak with good reason. When you look at the current unemployment rates for young people and also at the future prospects for European growth, it is hard to see what kind of a future lies ahead for European youth.

Moreover, when young people look at the fiscal policies of the generation that screwed up Europe, what they see is a mountain of debt that they are going to inherit. If you do any calculation about the future path of taxation for the next generation of employees — those who are lucky enough to be employed — the taxes are going to be far higher than they were in the last generation. We see this almost all the time, with the exodus of talented young Europeans to study in the United States. And it's really perceptible. This was already happening before the crisis, partly because of the bleak economic prospects, but also because the continental European universities have been rubbish since your generation screwed them up in 1968.

RUDYARD GRIFFITHS: Our final question from the stage is a good one because it's going to take this somewhat acrimonious foursome and force them to think in a new way.

BRITTANY TRUMPER: There has been a lot of great debating tonight, so what I want to know is, which of your opponents' arguments do you find the most compelling?

RUDYARD GRIFFITHS: This is going to be a bit of a mental shift for all of you. Josef?

JOSEF JOFFE: Peter, you defended something I totally agree with, which is that it is much better to have free trade and open borders than to have closed borders and no free trade. But that was not the issue of this debate.

The issue was whether Europe — the experiment — has failed. And the basic failure, I think, is that we have ground to a halt, and cannot continue. The reasons are deeply buried in our societies, in our social contracts and our political cultures, and above all in the fact that we are not one nation-state but twenty-seven separate nations with twenty-seven different histories and ways of doing things. And if you don't believe that these cultural differences can't be overcome, just look at the four of us, and the way we have debated here.

RUDYARD GRIFFITHS: So, Lord Mandelson, I'm going to have you end the question-and-answer session. Which of Niall's and Josef's arguments do you give credence to in the context of this discussion?

PETER MANDELSON: Well, I'm trying to give credence —

JOSEF JOFFE: But you haven't heard a good argument here, correct?

DANIEL COHN-BENDIT: You are like a little child.

RUDYARD GRIFFITHS: Gentlemen, let's not make this personal.

JOSEF JOFFE: But I don't agree with that one; I don't agree with that argument.

RUDYARD GRIFFITHS: Lord Mandelson, you have the final word here.

PETER MANDELSON: I am trying to give credence to Josef's argument that somehow we have achieved free trade across a 500-million-strong market in the European Union without anyone doing anything about it. Now, how do you think we came to create this market? It didn't happen by accident. It happened by political design. It's been built up over sixty years, and culminated in the creation of the single market in the late 1980s and the early 1990s. The architect of this design, by the way, was the then British commissioner in Brussels.[5] So thank you for all your sneering remarks about the British in Europe!

Josef, I want to ask you: would you rather see this fall apart? Would you rather dismantle it? Would you rather see a single market cease to exist? Because if you do, if you want to end what you call the European experiment, I would then have to put it back to you: how do you think

---

[5] Arthur Cockfield, Baron Cockfield (1916–2007), who resigned from Margaret Thatcher's cabinet to become a vice-president of the European Commission under Jacques Delors. Only months after beginning his tenure at the European Commission in 1985, he produced a white paper with 300 recommendations on how a single European market could be created.

business is going to grow? Considering the depth of the economic chaos that is going to blight Europe not for years, but for decades, where do you think jobs are going to come from? That's all I'm asking you to do.

I'm not denying that there are problems in the single currency. I've acknowledged those and I think they're very serious. But I happen to think that we can put them right. Niall disagrees; he thinks it is impossible; he thinks the Germans will always say no. I hope I've persuaded him that the Germans are actually in the middle of saying yes, but they want certain things to be put in place beforehand. They want a little more discipline, a few more rules, and they want a little more control over the eurozone before they start turning on the spending taps even more. I don't blame the Germans for asking for those things.

But to go back to my question for Josef. If you think this European experiment is so terrible, what effect do you think it would have on our economy, our businesses, and our jobs if we just let the whole thing fall apart?

JOSEF JOFFE: I didn't argue for letting it fall apart.

RUDYARD GRIFFITHS: Gentlemen. Let's move to closing statements. Lord Mandelson, because you just spoke, I'm going to change the order slightly. Daniel Cohn-Bendit, you're up first with your closing arguments. You have three minutes.

DANIEL COHN-BENDIT: I want to make this simple. I

completely agree that Europe and the single currency are having difficulties. I would sign my name to Niall Ferguson's article in the *Financial Times*. But we have to move forward. Our opponents say the problem is that Germany will say no. But Ms. Merkel wants to get a fiscal compact, and she needs a two-thirds majority. But she will need the votes of the Social Democrats and the Greens for this. And the Greens and the Social Democrats say that we have to take a step toward more solidarity and a redemption fund plan. Second, we need to take common responsibility for the future in countries like France, and we are going in this direction now. But this will be very difficult, knowing European history.

We are in a situation in Europe where the majority of the people want to move forward in union even if they are afraid. And Niall is right: France and Holland voted against the constitutional project; but we made a mistake. I never said Europe didn't make mistakes. However, the way out of the crisis is by deepening integration. This will take time and sometimes be challenging.

But to say the European project has failed moves us backwards. If you have scrambled eggs, you can't get the unbroken eggs back. If you have scrambled eggs, you have to try to divide them so that everybody can eat something. I want to say to everybody here: don't be fooled. Europe is a vision and a perspective; it is something very new considering our history; and I'm proud to say that I've put twenty years' work into this project.

I'm proud to say that I might have changed the history of Europe a little bit. Europeans have significant cultural differences today, but in thirty years the nation-state in Europe will cease to exist. And so there is a feeling amongst Europeans that we can be something in the future by working together. We will either be something together — and we will still own our cultural differences — or we will disappear as a political force entirely. And this is why I defend Europe.

RUDYARD GRIFFITHS: Josef Joffe, you're next with your closing remarks.

JOSEF JOFFE: Let me just dispense with the argument once and for all that Europe keeps the peace. That is historically and conceptually false. The problem is that security and peace were assured before we started integration. In fact, we couldn't have started integration unless there had been somebody else in the game, stronger than France, stronger than Germany, stronger than all the countries in Europe. That happened to be the United States, who protected each of the individual countries against the others and guaranteed everybody security. Once the security problem was solved, they could go on to build Europe.

I agree with the second point: the fact that Europe has to be part of the solution. We've just heard the two other debaters restating what is desirable and what should be. They rationalized why they will continue to defend Europe, and how it should go on and climb the north face of the Eiger, and so on. What neither of them has said is how this can be done, given that we are talking about twenty-seven nation-states.

Let me stick with the metaphor for a moment. Yes, I guess we could climb the cliff, but the problem is that we need somebody who leads and somebody who follows. And the problem with Europe is that most of us are just much better at saying no, *non*, or *nein* than at accepting anybody as a leader to rule the roost, and to rule the rest. If you look at it that way, then you will necessarily become more modest about what Europe should and can do. There is no Abraham Lincoln; there is no Count of Cavour;[6] there is no Bismarck, who can pummel and beat the rest into following him. And thank God for that, by the way. There are certain kinds of French deputies I would not want to be led by.

As for Peter's more prudent question, "Would you want to live in a Europe that is not Europe?" — that was not the issue of this debate. The issue of this debate was: has the experiment failed, and it seems to me that with some powers of observation the answer is yes. That does not mean we want to dismantle the whole thing. Nobody has argued that. Nobody in his right mind would argue for dismantling the union.

What happens next should be less ambitious; it should preserve what we have, while at the same time upholding the kind of realism that tells us that we are not going to be *E Pluribus Unum*.

RUDYARD GRIFFITHS: Lord Mandelson, your closing arguments, please.

---

[6] Camillo Benso, Count of Cavour (1810–1861), Piedmontese statesman who worked to bring about the unification of Italy; he became that country's first prime minister.

PETER MANDELSON: I don't expect people to show blind faith either in the euro, the single currency, or in the European project. What I do ask people, though, is not to accept the view of those who oppose this motion: that everything that is wrong in the eurozone and the operation of the single currency will remain wrong; that every mistake that has been made is irreversible — in other words, that all politics is hopeless. I'm asking you to accept the view that you can actually repair things, reverse mistakes, change things for the better.

I think that so much of what we've heard from the other side is, quite frankly, a sort of nihilistic council of despair. Now, I don't expect you to share my commitment to Europe, Niall. And I don't expect you to necessarily agree with my pro-European views — although, as I pointed out, you did do so three weeks ago in the *Financial Times*. What I ask you to do is just bear in mind what is at stake. This isn't a joke. We're talking about people's livelihoods; we're talking about people's jobs and their futures; we're talking about a whole generation of young people who need this to succeed, not fail. So please, stop praying and arguing for failure.

I'm not even saying that we will necessarily prevail. But for two reasons, all of us have got to make a huge, combined political effort to make this thing succeed and stay on its current path. One is that there would be no such thing as a Velvet Divorce in the eurozone: the fall-out would be absolutely tremendous for all of us on the continent. But second, and equally important, is that we're talking about the European Union as a whole, as a single economic space, which is the second largest of its kind in the world. It would not just be Europeans who would be hit if this thing fell apart. It would be people in advanced economies and developing economies, rich people and poor people, including many in Canada and right across the world.

That is why we have got to work together to help sort this out, and I believe that we can. It will take leadership, but there are leaders. There is leadership in Germany; there is a very good president who has just been elected in France. And while it is true that Britain is not, at the moment, at the forefront of Europe's leadership, I wish it were.

RUDYARD GRIFFITHS: Niall, you have the final word.

NIALL FERGUSON: In February of 2009, I gave an interview to the *Globe and Mail* in which I said that there would be blood; that in the wake of the financial crisis, there would be such political upheaval and social dislocation that the result would be violence. I believe that that prophecy is being fulfilled, and it is being fulfilled in large measure because of the failed experiment of European integration. My opponents have the direction of causation all wrong.

Why are there depression levels of unemployment in countries like Greece and Spain? It wasn't an act of God; it was a direct and predictable consequence of the failed experiment of monetary union — an experiment that was so obviously doomed to fail that your government elected not to join the euro, Peter. If the British were such big believers in European integration, why was it that year after year the Labour government refused to join? You know the answer. The answer was that at least some people in your party, including your old friend, former prime minster Gordon Brown, saw what was coming.

The magnitude of the crisis that is being inflicted on the European periphery by this failed experiment can hardly be overstated. And the stakes are very high. We could be on the brink of a second phase of depression. If this thing turns into a bank run that sweeps right through the Mediterranean region, it could be 1931 all over again. And what happens after that? What happens if the worst-case scenario takes place? What happens if the Germans continue to say no to the kinds of federal measures that might possibly staunch the flow of money out of Spanish banks?

Other experiments are also failing in Europe right now: the experiment of the excessively generous welfare state and the experiment of multiculturalism, which has created huge ghettoes of unconnected immigrants, who are the most likely to be the focal point for the populist backlash that is in the pipeline. The experiment has been more dangerous than any of the eurocrats have ever admitted, and we will see the full consequences when the laboratory blows up.

The great Viennese satirist Karl Kraus once described the Habsburg Empire as an experimental laboratory for world destruction. My fear, ladies and gentlemen, is that this is what the European Union is poised to become. This experiment has failed. Thank you.

RUDYARD GRIFFITHS: Ladies and gentlemen, let me just reiterate something Peter Munk has said at past debates. It's one thing to give a set piece speech in front of a large audience — speakers of such quality and calibre as the men on the stage tonight do it all the time. It is something quite different, though, to put your ideas forward, to have them contested the way they have been tonight, and frankly to talk about an issue that is, again, hardly academic. This affects the lives of hundreds of millions of people, possibly even the future of the global economy. It's been a spirited debate that has given us all a larger understanding of Europe, as well as an enriched conversation. So please join me in a round of applause and appreciation for our debaters.

Summary: The pre-debate vote was 41 percent in favour of the resolution; 37 percent against; and 22 percent undecided. The final vote showed a disappearance of the undecided voters, with 45 percent in favour of the motion and 55 percent against it. Given the shift in votes, the victory goes to the team arguing against the resolution, Lord Peter Mandelson and Daniel Cohn-Bendit.

NIALL FERGUSON IN CONVERSATION
WITH SONIA VERMA

SONIA VERMA: Thank you so much for joining us. I thought that I would start by getting your response to the resolution that will be debated tonight. Can you discuss the resolution: be it resolved the European experiment has failed?

NIALL FERGUSON: You only need to turn on the TV or open your newspaper to see the European experiment failing, in the sense that monetary union is ending with a colossal financial debacle, as some of us predicted it would. I've just come from Europe where the situation's pretty grave. If Greece leaves the monetary union, nobody actually knows what the ramifications will be, but the most likely scenario is a major run on the Spanish banks, since people fear Spain may be next to fall.

I think the wider question that will be debated tonight

is whether the whole project of European integration, dating back to the 1950s, has failed. And I'm sure there will be a case to be made on the other side that this has gone better than Europe before 1945: it would be pretty hard to argue otherwise. Remember, however, that the reason there has been peace in Europe since the 1950s has had very little to do with the European Union and everything to do with NATO; it has had everything to do with the fact that Europeans did not pool their military sovereignty, but accepted American military leadership during and after the Cold War. So we have to make sure we don't get into an argument about war and peace — that's not what European integration has been about. It's been about economics. And I'm going to argue that in economic terms, European integration has failed to deliver the promised growth, the promised jobs, and the promised prosperity.

SONIA VERMA: Let's talk about the crisis itself, because I think you have a unique perspective, having just returned from Europe. You spent some time in Spain, I think. What did you see? What's the mood there? What was the atmosphere like? What are Spaniards saying?

NIALL FERGUSON: The first thing I encountered was a large protest in the streets of Barcelona against the austerity measures that the new Spanish government is having to take. There is constant discussion among ordinary Spaniards about whether or not to leave their money in Spanish banks. There is a great deal of anxiety surrounding the fate of a bank called Bankia, a large and obviously insolvent institution, that has just been taken over by the Spanish government. The mood is bleak. If you look at youth unemployment in Spain, it's 50 percent. Young people are leaving Spain and seeking their fortunes elsewhere. So if you want an example of a place where the European experiment is failing pretty disastrously, take a trip to Spain.

SONIA VERMA: I'm going to ask you to look into your crystal ball and predict the outcome of this current crisis. What do you think is the right outcome? What is the most disastrous outcome that we could face?

NIALL FERGUSON: If you had asked me a couple of weeks ago, I would have said that there is no way that anybody gains from Greece leaving the monetary union. I would have said, they're going to come to an agreement on eurobonds that integrates the fiscal systems, so that the full faith and credit of the European Union stands behind the national debts, or at least some of the national debts. And I would have confidently predicted that an agreement would be reached on Europe-wide deposit insurance to take the heat off the Spanish banks. Having travelled around Europe over the last couple of weeks, I'm a lot less optimistic because what I see is a worsening crisis on the periphery, and complacency at the core.

Unfortunately, the German government, led by Angela Merkel, is extremely reluctant to take the steps that, I believe, are necessary to avoid a major financial crisis, despite coming under substantial pressure from the French, Italian, and Spanish governments. Until the German government softens its stance and shows itself more ready to contemplate eurobonds — meaning some measure of fiscal integration or federalism at the heart of the European Union — we are in a very dangerous place. And I would say this bears comparison with the summer of 1931, when the depression entered its second phase; when Creditanstalt, a big Austrian bank, went bust and set off a chain reaction of bank failures. The Europeans are playing with fire — or, I should really say, the Germans are playing with fire, because right now it is up to the German government to decide where we go. We can either go down the route of fiscal federalism, which was always implicit in the monetary union project, or we can go down the route of European disintegration starting with Greece, but by no means stopping with Greece.

SONIA VERMA: How do you make the case to the German people that this idea of fiscal federalism is something that would actually benefit them? Germany's economy is doing much better compared to the peripheral economies of Spain and Greece. So what's in it for them?

NIALL FERGUSON: There are two ways of making this case. The first is to say to Germany that you've been the principal beneficiaries of the monetary union. If you had stayed outside of the euro — if you had stayed with the Deutschmark — you would have experienced the problems the Swiss experienced with an overvalued currency in the crisis, so you should be more appreciative of what monetary union has done for you. But I don't actually think you're ever going to convince Germans with arguments like that. You have to appeal to fear rather than to altruism.

Here is the reality. Already because of the way European financial integration has proceeded, and the way the crisis has unfolded, three to four to five hundred billion euros are owed to Germany by the peripheral Mediterranean economies, through something called Target2, which is the European payments mechanism. If those Mediterranean countries leave the eurozone, there will be a massive default on those Target2 liabilities because they would be converted unilaterally by the exit into drachmas, pesetas, escudos, or lire. So the Germans are on the hook one way or the other; they can choose how to pay. They can pay through Mediterranean defaults and the breakup of the monetary union, as well as the subsequent effects of returning to the Deutschmark, which would be very macroeconomically disruptive and would affect everybody, including Canada and certainly the United States; or they can pay through transfers like the ones that they've been making to East Germany since the 1990s. They are big transfers — it's not going to be cheap. Canadians understand federalism, and that it's always painful when money has to pass from one state to another. But from my point of view, it is a far preferable way for Germany to pay for Europe than to pay for it through a huge banking crisis on the periphery or through serial defaults.

SONIA VERMA: What about this issue of political instability in some European countries, like France? Or what about the deadlock in Greece? A lot of these countries are going through a lot of internal strife politically — their governments aren't able to rule: so how will any kind of federalism or supranational organization emerge from that sort of chaos?

NIALL FERGUSON: When you look at the latest Greek opinion polls, it superficially seems as if things are going to hell in a handcart. There is a possibility that a new government will be formed, led by a party that rejects all of the commitments the Greeks entered into to get their bailout; and it's not just Greece that has a problem. In fact, take a tour of many European governments and what you'll find is disarray. Disarray in the Netherlands, disarray in Belgium — it's not just the Mediterranean countries that have a political problem. It seems as if there is no such thing as a two-term government in Europe anymore. You're only elected for one term because you are bound to disappoint your supporters in that one term.

However, I think there is another way of thinking about this: the worse it gets at the national level, the more plausible a federal solution becomes. I think part of what we are seeing here are protest votes against national politicians. We certainly saw that in Greece. It's not that they are actually voting against the euro — if you actually look at the positions of the parties, almost nobody in Greece favours an exit from the euro; but Greek voters are very, very aggrieved, and they blame the major parties of the last ten years, including the Panhellenic Socialist Movement and New Democracy, for the mess that they are in. So they punish them by voting for these new populist parties, either on the Left or the Right. I think this is the prelude to a federal outcome.

One way of thinking about this is to look at Italy. Italians despise their national politicians — regard them all as crooks or depraved playboys, as in the case of Silvio Berlusconi. Italians are also the most pro-European of Europeans: they have the highest ratings of European institutions in the Eurobarometer polls. So, my hypothesis is that the worse it gets at the national level, the closer you get to a federal outcome. Because who are the respected politicians in Europe? People like Mario Monti, former European commissioner, now prime minister of Italy; these politicians are respected — the technocrats, not the local party hacks.

SONIA VERMA: Speaking of public sentiment, Ipsos carried out a poll commissioned by the Munk Debates that showed what you were just talking about: that most Europeans don't want to leave the euro. What does that speak to, from your perspective?

NIALL FERGUSON: I think it's important to recognize that

from the vantage point of electorates, European integration is still a worthy project, preferable to the bad old days of nation-states, despite all the economic problems we are seeing in Europe at the moment. And I think if you're Greece and you were asked, "Would you like to go back in time, to the days of high inflation and even military dictatorship?" or "Would you like to stick with the gains that have come to you since you joined the EU?" the Greeks would overwhelmingly say, "We'll stick with the EU." The past isn't an attractive place for Spain, either. Remember, for countries like Spain, Portugal, and Greece, pre-Europe was a time of dictatorship. And that is one reason why there is so little popular appetite for breaking up this thing.

The trouble is that the elites who run Europe thought that they could back the European peoples into a federal system through a kind of reverse takeover where you do the monetary union first, which then somewhat forces you into a federal union. I don't think that was clever because it hasn't been popular, and it's had very bad economic effects. What you have in Europe right now is disillusioned Europeans, not people who are anxious to return to their old nation-states. That's why I think this thing is still more likely to hang together. But, as I said earlier, it desperately needs the Germans to see the logic of fiscal federalism, which was always implicit in the project of monetary union.

SONIA VERMA: In many ways, you actually predicted the current crisis ten years ago. You said this would happen.

How does it make you feel to have seen this mess unfolding in advance?

NIALL FERGUSON: Let me get the timing right here. Actually, I was critical of the project of monetary union right through the 1990s, when it was being thrashed out. I opposed it in 1992, at the time of the Maastricht Treaty. When the monetary union came into existence I warned, very explicitly, where this would lead. And in 2000, I published a piece in *Foreign Affairs* with my good friend Larry Kotlikoff, in which we explained that a monetary union without fiscal union would fall apart after about ten years because of the divergence between the member states — and that is exactly what we are seeing. Now I should really be running around doing a victory lap, punching the air and gloating, chanting "I told you so" from the rooftops, but that's not really how I feel. The way I feel now is that we really do have to try and knock some sense into the key decision-makers — not only the politicians, but also the bankers. To make them realize just how high the stakes are.

If this thing goes wrong, it affects everybody, including the people who were right about monetary union, like me. I don't really want to see the world economy hit, at this stage — five years since the onset of the financial crisis — by a European bank run, and potentially by a whole spate of European defaults. I think that would be hugely disruptive for the global economic recovery, and it would affect the economies on this side of the Atlantic almost as severely as it would affect countries like

Germany. So I'm running around Europe — it's rather exhausting, I have to say — trying to communicate some historical insight to decision-makers, and trying to remind them that what made the Great Depression great was a massive European banking crisis in the summer of 1931. And this is the summer of 1931 for our generation. It's up to the decision-makers, especially in Berlin but also in Brussels, to avoid repeating that catastrophe of the Great Depression.

PETER MANDELSON IN CONVERSATION
WITH SONIA VERMA

SONIA VERMA: First of all, thank you so much for joining us for this interview. Everyone is very much looking
forward to the debate. I thought I would start by asking you for your response to the resolution that is being
debated tonight. Can you discuss the resolution: be it
resolved the European experiment has failed?

PETER MANDELSON: Well, it depends on how you define
failure. I mean, yes, we have stumbled in the creation of
our single currency in Europe, but that, in my view, was
due to problems of design and execution, not concept
or principle. If you step back and look at what Europe
has achieved in the last sixty years of its life, we have
successfully, by any measure, road-tested a model of
supranationalism that doesn't exist anywhere in the
world; it doesn't have a precedent in history.

If you look at the direction of our travel, and our achievement, you will see twenty-seven countries in Europe that have transformed the way they relate to each other in their economics, their trade, their commerce; how they conduct their diplomatic relations with the rest of the world; and how they co-ordinate many areas of important policy for Europeans — and the impact those policies have on the rest of the world.

None of that is being put in question or doubt by the fact that — and I fully accept this — we have stumbled on the implementation of the single currency. If you are asking me, however, whether the single currency is doomed to fail, I would say no. If you are asking me whether we should have done things differently from the beginning in organizing it, my answer would certainly be yes. And if you also ask me whether I believe the single currency in its operation can be repaired, and it can be worked differently, I too believe the answer to that question is yes; but it's going to involve some pain, a lot of focus, and a lot of political will and determination to put it right.

SONIA VERMA: I want to go back a little bit in history. Of course, with the benefit of hindsight, you talk about things that you know could have been done differently, with an emphasis specifically on political institutions. How do you think we could have avoided the current crisis?

PETER MANDELSON: In the 1990s, when all the parts of the single currency of economic and monetary union were coming together, some people said we were over-ambitious; that we were trying to run economically before we could walk politically. But I actually look at it rather differently. I think there was a lack of ambition. I think that we should have been more ambitious in creating the fiscal and the political union that are needed to make a currency zone work effectively.

All of these issues of how far we came together in the integration of our fiscal policies, and the implications of a more centralized political management of the whole project, were sensitive in the 1990s. It was easier to duck those difficult questions, and to assume that somehow the whole thing would emerge in due course, or that it would all come out in the wash. Now we have faced and experienced the financial crash of 2008, which was a huge external shock. And in the wake of that crisis, the design and implementation weaknesses of the eurozone were exposed in a rather raw way, and that's what we are having to come to terms with now.

SONIA VERMA: I wanted to ask you about the potential way out of the current crisis. I think you and your opponents actually agree about the depth of how bad things are, specifically in countries like Greece, Spain, and Italy. But given where we are right now, what do you see as the best outcome? How do we get past this stalemate that European leaders seem to be locked into right now?

PETER MANDELSON: Well, I think the people I'm debating with will be saying the whole thing was doomed for failure; that it was all the fault of visionary politicians who were completely out of touch with reality and with public opinion; and it was the madcap elite with some grandiose project who tried to impose it on everyone else. Actually, the single currency was not like that. The euro was seen as a natural extension of the huge economic space that we had created through the single market in Europe. The single currency was about making our economic relations, doing business, and how we trade and undertake commerce easier and less costly. And that's what I mean when I say that the principle was right even if the implementation was flawed.

Those same people will probably say that it has all been a disaster, so let's break the thing up and revert to our own national currencies. I'm afraid that would not be easy. It would be colossally painful for our economies. I think it would create an economic disaster with social consequences that would blight not just Europe for years, and possibly decades, to come. I don't believe that reversal could simply be achieved by a sort of flick of the switch, or flourish of a pen. We have to understand that Europe's economic space, and what this represents, is huge: it is the second biggest economic bloc of its kind in the world. We have the largest banking sector in the world. If European banks simply plunged into chaos and disorder, it would be felt not just in Europe, but by the rest of the world — and that would be, in my view, a very irresponsible course of action for us to take.

SONIA VERMA: How do we move forward, though? What is lacking from the leaders of Europe today that's really prevented any progress out of the debt crisis that's been just hanging over the eurozone?

PETER MANDELSON: It is not true to say that there's been no progress. The ways in which European member states in the currency zone have come to terms with the debt crisis, how they've adapted, and the policy responses they've put together are considerable; they are, frankly, greater, and have happened more quickly, than one might have foreseen at the beginning of the crisis.

But there is still a great deal more to do. In my view, for example, you have to have fiscal and monetary policies, collective policies for the eurozone as a whole — centrally managed and conducted — that imply a degree of fiscal and political union that doesn't exist in the eurozone at the moment. Secondly, the European Central Bank has to assume a greater role and responsibility. I think people, including the markets, somehow assume that when we created this currency zone, it was a single sort of political entity with a central bank that would act as the lender of last resort; that it would stand behind the currency and sovereign debt, as you have in Canada, or they have in the United States with the Federal Reserve. But, very deliberately, the European Central Bank was not originally created with that role. Now, in my view, that has to change. I also think there has to be some joint responsibility for sovereign debt as a whole.

SONIA VERMA: Are you suggesting the idea of eurobonds?

PETER MANDELSON: Yes, I am. And the banking system in Europe, as a whole. There has to be a sort of collective sharing of responsibility for that debt and for the capitalization of banks, which require important steps forward in how the eurozone operates and the further steps of integration that it has to undergo. This is not easy.

For Germany, as an example, it implies an almost unlimited exposure to the costs and liabilities of the eurozone. Germany — for all its strength, for all that it has done, the hit the country has taken, and the burden it has amassed by dealing with the crisis to the extent that it has over the last year or two — is still not yet ready to take those further steps. I think Germany will do it, eventually, but it has to take its people and its public with it. Germany is a country with a very strong constitutional accord. I'm afraid that in Germany it is not really just for the chancellor or the government to pull levers, or turn switches. There is a German Parliament, there is a German constitutional accord; there are the German people, who have all got to be convinced to make these changes and go in this direction.

I think they will, because the continuation of the single currency is far too important to Germans for them to lose it. They realize that it represents a huge commitment by them to the whole of the European project, which they want to sustain. They also know how important it is for the rest of the world. But time, unlimited time, is not at our disposal, and many of us would like to see these political decisions and changes being made more speedily. But they are underway; we just need to pick up the pace.

SONIA VERMA: How do you do that in a country like Germany, which is fairly prosperous? There is a huge disparity between the economy of Germany and the economy of Greece. How do you make that case to the German people, who you ultimately need to convince?

PETER MANDELSON: I think you make that case in this way. First of all, you point to Germany's own experience. Germany was two Germanys, you know, and they came together and reunited. It involved merging the two economies, creating a single currency between two parts of Germany, West and East, which were very, very different. This has involved a huge transfer of resources, which is continuing today. It has involved great changes — structural changes — to labour and other markets in Germany, to the welfare system, how people work, how hard they work, and with what reward. And the German people, it is true, embraced these changes, which involved considerable sacrifice. But what they see is an outcome, a larger German economy, which is giving them — in other respects — enormous benefits and enormous rewards. And my second point is that everyone in Germany knows that the country has been the principal beneficiary in the creation of economic and monetary union.

SONIA VERMA: Can you explain that a little bit more?

PETER MANDELSON: Well, Germany has created an evaluation of the euro, which has benefited German exports; they've created a market for the currency to operate. The euro has allowed Germans to trade and supply their goods and services within Europe and overseas very successfully, with great benefits for the German economy, and the German people. Germany — as an economic powerhouse — has been ready and better able to take advantage of low borrowing costs than Greece or Portugal, for example, or some of the eurozone countries in the southern perimeter. And that, at its heart, is the problem.

When the single currency was created, there was an expectation, central to the plan, that with these rather diverse economies — with their varying levels of productivity and competitiveness — there would be benefits and opportunities through the single currency. But there was also a belief that there would be discipline to bring about a convergence of these disparate economies in the single currency, that Greece would become more like Germany — but in fact the opposite has happened. They didn't take advantage of the opportunities, and they didn't respond to the discipline of the single currency. Cruelly, perhaps you might say, they took the free lunch without understanding the bill would have to be paid for that lunch. And rather than the convergence of these economies, we've seen a divergence. Now, that has got to be changed for the eurozone to be put on an enduring successful basis.

People who talk rather glibly say, "Well, we can just lose Greece," or "We could just revert to national currencies where we want," or "Germany can provide a core and everyone else can just go off and do their own thing." I say we are too integrated; we are too far gone down the course for that to be done quickly, simply, or painlessly. The alternative to repair the shortcomings is not just an institutional question of creating a stronger basis of political and fiscal union in the single currency. It is also a question of transferring a lot of resources, and making a lot of fiscal transfers to those countries that have not only to recover from the immediate crisis that they are undergoing, but have got to use that investment to transform their economies so that they start converging with the rest of the eurozone rather than continuing to diverge.

SONIA VERMA: In the sea of bad news coming out of Europe, you come across as a bit of an optimist. What are your reasons are for being so optimistic?

PETER MANDELSON: I hope that in my optimism, you don't think I'm being completely unrealistic. I'm not saying that there are any easy options: no course that we take to get out of this crisis is going to be a walk in the park. It's not going to be plain sailing, believe me. And as the old Chinese motto goes, we are going to have to eat a great deal of bitterness in order to dig ourselves out of this crisis — to both right and stabilize the eurozone, and to put it on a workable, sustainable basis and course for the future. I'm not saying that we are bound to do that, but I am saying that we can do it.

I disagree with those who believe that the whole thing was completely misconceived and is incapable of working properly. If you look at the polling that has been undertaken by the *Globe and Mail* in Europe, you'll see that across Europe, to varying degrees, people want to retain the single currency despite everything they are going through. They want the currency to be repaired, and they want the currency union to continue into the future. But it is the job of the politicians to listen to the public. Politicians have to accept their shortcomings and the mistakes they have made. I suppose, indirectly, I was one of them: I was the European Union's commissioner for trade. I played my part in how this was handled, although I did so more latterly than at the beginning, just to get my excuses in. They are right to be angry with their politicians. Greeks are right to be angry with their political and economic system, as a whole. But once you've got through your anger, you then have to do something to put things right. And it's the politicians' job to lead properly. They should not give false optimism, but they need to hold their nerves nonetheless, and be confident that what we have to do, we can do — as long as we do it in a united way and do it together.

SONIA VERMA: Thank you so much for your time, I really appreciate it.

PETER MANDELSON: Thank you.

ACKNOWLEDGEMENTS

The Munk Debates are the product of the public-spiritedness of a remarkable group of civic-minded organizations and individuals. First and foremost, these debates would not be possible without the vision and leadership of the Aurea Foundation. Founded in 2006 by Peter and Melanie Munk, the Aurea Foundation supports Canadian individuals and institutions involved in the study and development of public policy. The debates are the foundation's signature initiative, a model for the kind of substantive public policy conversation Canadians can foster globally. Since their creation in 2008, the foundation has underwritten the entire cost of each semi-annual debate. The debates have also benefited from the input and advice of members of the board of foundation, including Mark Cameron, Andrew Coyne, Devon Cross, Allan Gotlieb, George Jonas, Margaret MacMillan, Anthony Munk, and Janice Stein.

For her contribution to the preliminary edit of the book, the debate organizers would like to thank Jane McWhinney.

Since their inception the Munk Debates have sought to take the discussions that happen at each event to national and international audiences. Here the debates have benefited immeasurably from a partnership with Canada's national newspaper, the *Globe and Mail*, and the counsel of its editor-in-chief John Stackhouse.

With the publication of this superb book, House of Anansi Press is helping the debates reach new audiences in Canada and internationally. The debates' organizers would like to thank Anansi chair, Scott Griffin, and president and publisher, Sarah MacLachlan, for their enthusiasm for this book project and insights into how to translate the spoken debate into a powerful written intellectual exchange.

ABOUT THE DEBATERS

DANIEL COHN-BENDIT is a French-born German politician who rose to public prominence as a leader of the student revolts in France in the 1960s. He has remained a highly influential voice in Europe, serving as co-president of the Greens/European Free Alliance Group in the European Parliament since 2002. He sits on the parliamentary committees for Economic and Monetary Affairs and Constitutional Affairs. Cohn-Bendit is also co-chair of the Spinelli Group, a European Parliament initiative dedicated to the federalist project in Europe.

NIALL FERGUSON is the Laurence A. Tisch Professor of History at Harvard University and William Ziegler Professor of Business Administration at Harvard Business School. He is also a Senior Research Fellow at Jesus College, Oxford University, and a Senior Fellow at the Hoover Institution, Stanford University. He is the author of numerous bestselling books, including *Empire: The Rise and Demise of the British World Order and the Lessons for Global Power*, *The Ascent of Money: A Financial History of the World*, and *Civilization: The West and the Rest*. A prolific commentator on contemporary politics and economics, Ferguson is a contributing editor for Bloomberg TV and a weekly columnist with *Newsweek*.

JOSEF JOFFE is publisher-editor of the German weekly *Die Zeit*. He is a regular contributor to the *Wall Street Journal*, *New York Times*, *Washington Post*, *TIME*, and *Newsweek*. He is the author of numerous nonfiction books, including *Überpower: The Imperial Temptation of America*. In 2005, he co-founded the foreign policy journal *The American Interest* with Francis Fukuyama and Zbigniew Brzezinski. Joffe is also a Senior Fellow at Stanford University's Institute for International Studies, and has taught at Harvard, John Hopkins, and the University of Munich.

PETER MANDELSON is a member of the House of Lords and chairman of Global Counsel, a strategic advisory firm. He was elected to Parliament in 1992 and entered the British government in 1997, serving as secretary of state for trade and industry and secretary of state for Northern Ireland. From 2004 to 2008, he was the EU commissioner for trade. He re-entered the British government in 2008, serving as secretary of state for business, innovation, and skills. Mandelson is also a bestselling author: his autobiography, *The Third Man*, was a *Sunday Times* number-one bestseller for five consecutive weeks.

ABOUT THE EDITOR

RUDYARD GRIFFITHS is the organizer and moderator of the Munk Debates. In 2006 he was named one of Canada's "Top 40 under 40" by the *Globe and Mail*. He is the editor of thirteen books on history, politics, and international affairs, including *Who We Are: A Citizen's Manifesto*, which was a *Globe and Mail* Best Book of 2009 and a finalist for the Shaughnessy Cohen Prize for Political Writing. He lives in Toronto with his wife and two children.

ABOUT THE MUNK DEBATES

The Munk Debates are Canada's premier public policy event. Held semi-annually, the debates provide leading thinkers with a global forum to discuss the major public policy issues facing the world and Canada. Each event takes place in Toronto in front of a live audience, and the proceedings are covered by domestic and international media. Participants in recent Munk Debates include Robert Bell, Tony Blair, John Bolton, Ian Bremmer, Paul Collier, Howard Dean, Hernando de Soto, Gareth Evans, Mia Farrow, Niall Ferguson, William Frist, David Gratzer, Rick Hillier, Christopher Hitchens, Richard Holbrooke, Henry Kissinger, Charles Krauthammer, Paul Krugman, Lord Nigel Lawson, Stephen Lewis, David Li, Bjørn Lomborg, Elizabeth May, George Monbiot, Dambisa Moyo, Samantha Power, David Rosenberg, Lawrence Summers, and Fareed Zakaria.

The Munk Debates are a project of the Aurea

Foundation, a charitable organization established in 2006 by philanthropists Peter and Melanie Munk to promote public policy research and discussion. For more information visit www.munkdebates.com.

PERMISSIONS

North America's Lost Decade?

Krugman and Rosenberg vs. Summers and Bremmer

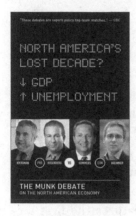

The future of the North American economy is more uncertain than ever. In this edition of the Munk Debates, Nobel Prize-winning economist Paul Krugman and Chief Economist and Strategist at Gluskin Sheff + Associates David Rosenberg square off against former U.S. Treasury Secretary Lawrence Summers and bestselling author Ian Bremmer to tackle the resolution: be it resolved North America faces a Japan-style era of high unemployment and slow growth.

"It's now impossible to deny the obvious, which is that we are not now, and have never been, on the road to recovery."
— Paul Krugman

Does the 21st Century Belong to China?
Kissinger and Zakaria vs. Ferguson and Li

Is China's rise unstoppable? Former U.S. Secretary of State Henry Kissinger and CNN's Fareed Zakaria pair off against leading historian Niall Ferguson and world-renowned Chinese economist David Daokui Li to debate China's emergence as a global force, the key geopolitical issue of our time.

This edition of the Munk Debates also features the first formal public debate Dr. Kissinger has participated in on China's future.

"I have enormous difficulty imagining a world dominated by China ... I believe the concept that any one country will dominate the world is, in itself, a misunderstanding of the world in which we live now." — Henry Kissinger

Hitchens vs. Blair

Christopher Hitchens vs. Tony Blair

Intellectual juggernaut and staunch atheist Christopher Hitchens goes head-to-head with former British Prime Minister Tony Blair, one of the Western world's most openly devout political leaders, on the age-old question: is religion a force for good in the world? Few world leaders have had a greater hand in shaping current events than Blair; few writers have been more outspoken and polarizing than Hitchens.

Sharp, provocative, and thoroughly engrossing, *Hitchens vs. Blair* is a rigorous and electrifying intellectual sparring match on the contentious questions that continue to dog the topic of religion in our globalized world.

"If religious instruction were not allowed until the child had attained the age of reason, we would be living in a very different world." — Christopher Hitchens

www.houseofanansi.com/munkdebates

The Munk Debates: Volume One
Edited by Rudyard Griffiths; Introduction by Peter Munk

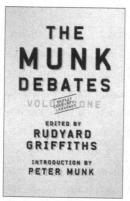

Launched in 2008 by philanthropists Peter and Melanie Munk, the Munk Debates is Canada's premier international debate series, a highly anticipated cultural event that brings together the world's brightest minds.

This volume includes the first five debates in the series, and features twenty leading thinkers and doers arguing for or against provocative resolutions that address pressing public policy concerns, such as the future of global security, the implications of humanitarian intervention, the effectiveness of foreign aid, the threat of climate change, and the state of health care in Canada and the United States.

"By trying to highlight the most important issues at crucial moments in the global conversation, these debates not only profile the ideas and solutions of some of our brightest thinkers and doers, but crystallize public passion and knowledge, helping to tackle some global challenges confronting humankind."
— Peter Munk
www.houseofanansi.com/munkdebates